LATINAS

IN THEIR OWN Words

LATINAS EN SUS PALABRAS

Art by Hanna Barczyk

SCHOLASTIC INC.

RIGOBERTA MENCHÚ

(1959)

Rigoberta Menchú nació en Aldea Chimel, Guatemala. Durante su niñez fue trabajadora migrante en el campo y más tarde se convirtió en luchadora por los derechos de las mujeres y los pueblos indígenas. En 1992, Menchú ganó el Premio Nobel de la Paz por su trabajo en defensa de los pueblos indígenas.

Rigoberta Menchú was born in Aldea Chimel, Guatemala. She spent her childhood as a migrant worker and became an advocate for the rights of women and indigenous people. In 1992 Menchú won the Nobel Peace Prize for her advocacy work for indigenous people.

Nuestra historia es una historia viva, que ha palpitado, resistido y sobrevivido siglos de sacrificios.

Our history is a living history, that has throbbed, withstood and survived many centuries of sacrifice.

JULIA DE BURGOS

(1914–1953)

Julia de Burgos fue una poeta que nació en Carolina, Puerto Rico. En sus escritos llamó por la independencia de Puerto Rico y la igualdad de la mujer. Era una orgullosa afro-puertorriqueña y una de las escritoras más importantes del siglo veinte.

Julia de Burgos was a poet born in Carolina, Puerto Rico. Through her writings she advocated for Puerto Rico's independence and women's equality. She was a proud Afro-Puerto Rican and one of the most important writers of the 20th century.

Yo soy la vida, la fuerza,
la mujer.

I am life, I am strength,
I am woman.

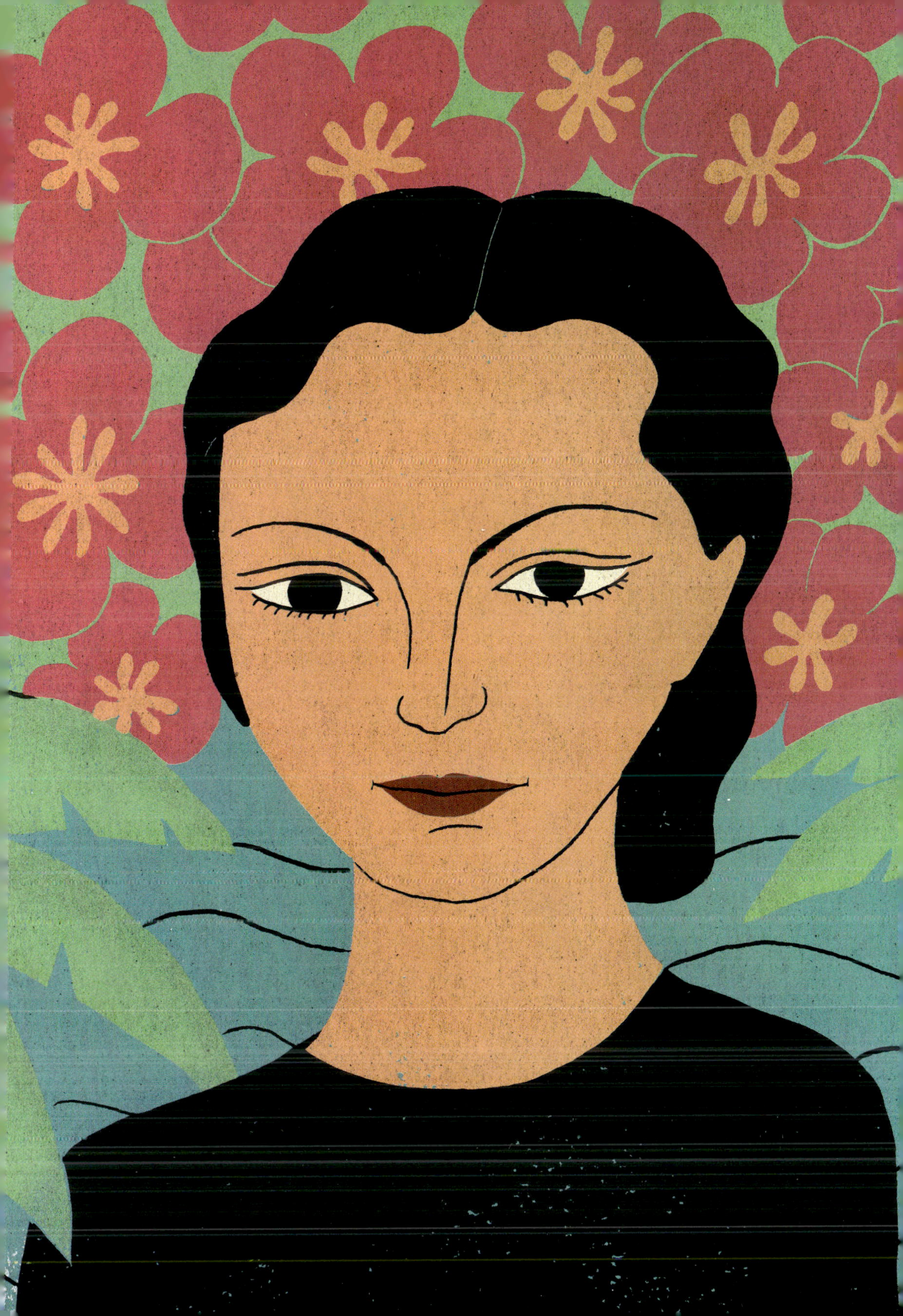

PURA BELPRÉ

(1899–1982)

Pura Belpré nació en Cidra, Puerto Rico y fue la primera bibliotecaria puertorriqueña de la biblioteca pública de Nueva York. Adquirió los primeros libros en español para la colección. En 1966 el Premio Pura Belpré se estableció en su honor para celebrar las contribuciones de los latinos a la literatura infantil.

Born in Cidra, Puerto Rico, Pura Belpré was the New York Public Library's first Puerto Rican librarian. She acquired the first Spanish-language books for the collection. In 1966 the Pura Belpré Award was established in her honor to celebrate the contributions of Latinos to children's literature.

A través del poder de una historia y la belleza del lenguaje, el niño escapa a su propio mundo. Sale de la habitación más rico que cuando entró.

Through the power of a story and the beauty of its language, the child escapes to a world of his own. He leaves the room richer than when he entered it.

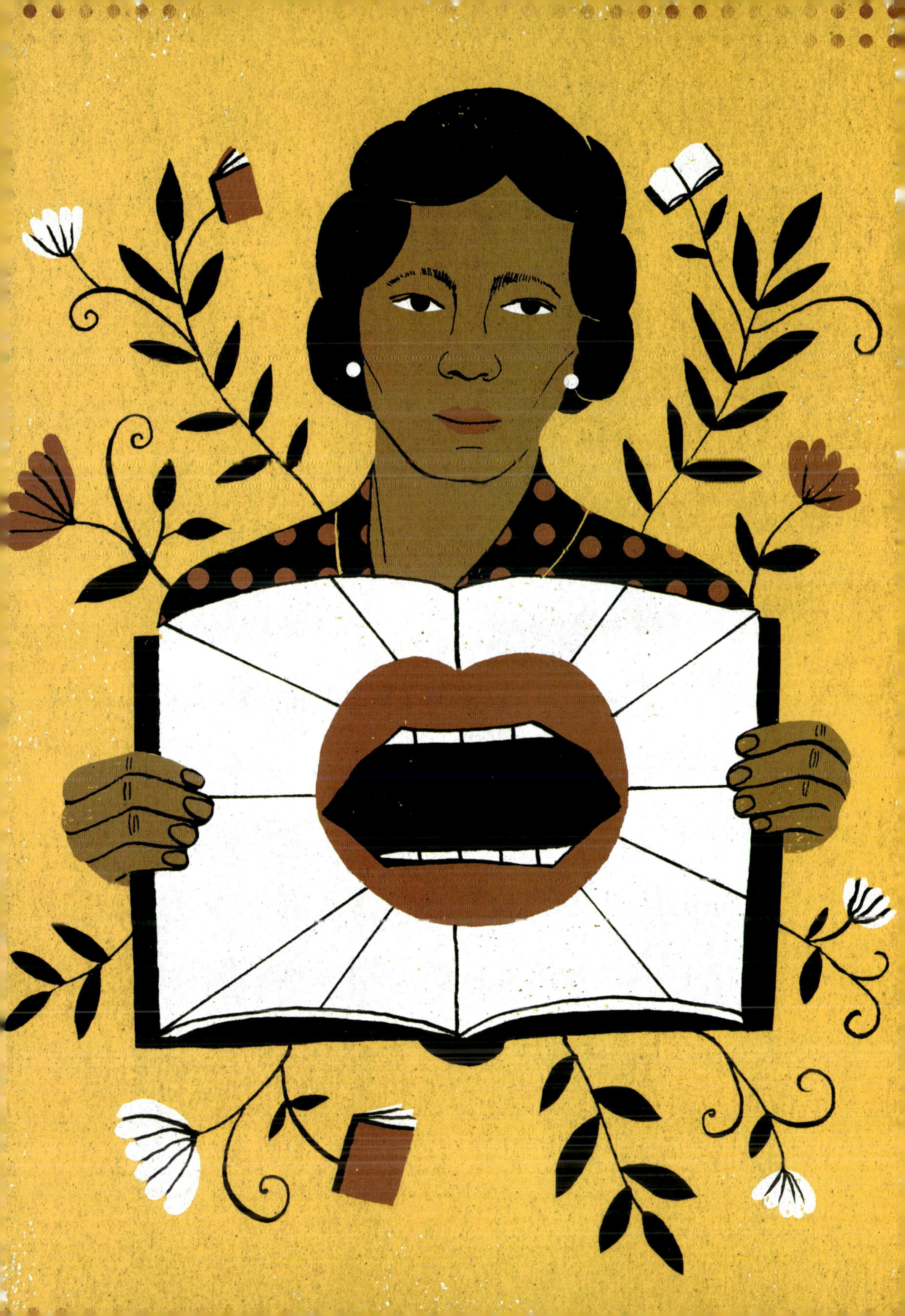

CHAVELA VARGAS

(1919–2012)

Chavela Vargas nació en San Joaquín de Flores, Costa Rica. Más tarde se mudó a México y revolucionó la música ranchera como mujer gay que desafiaba los roles tradicionales de género.

Chavela Vargas was born in San Joaquin de Flores, Costa Rica. Later in life she moved to Mexico and revolutionized ranchera music as a gay women who challenged traditional gender roles.

Uno vuelve siempre
a los viejos sitios donde
amó la vida.

One always returns
to those old places
where we loved life.

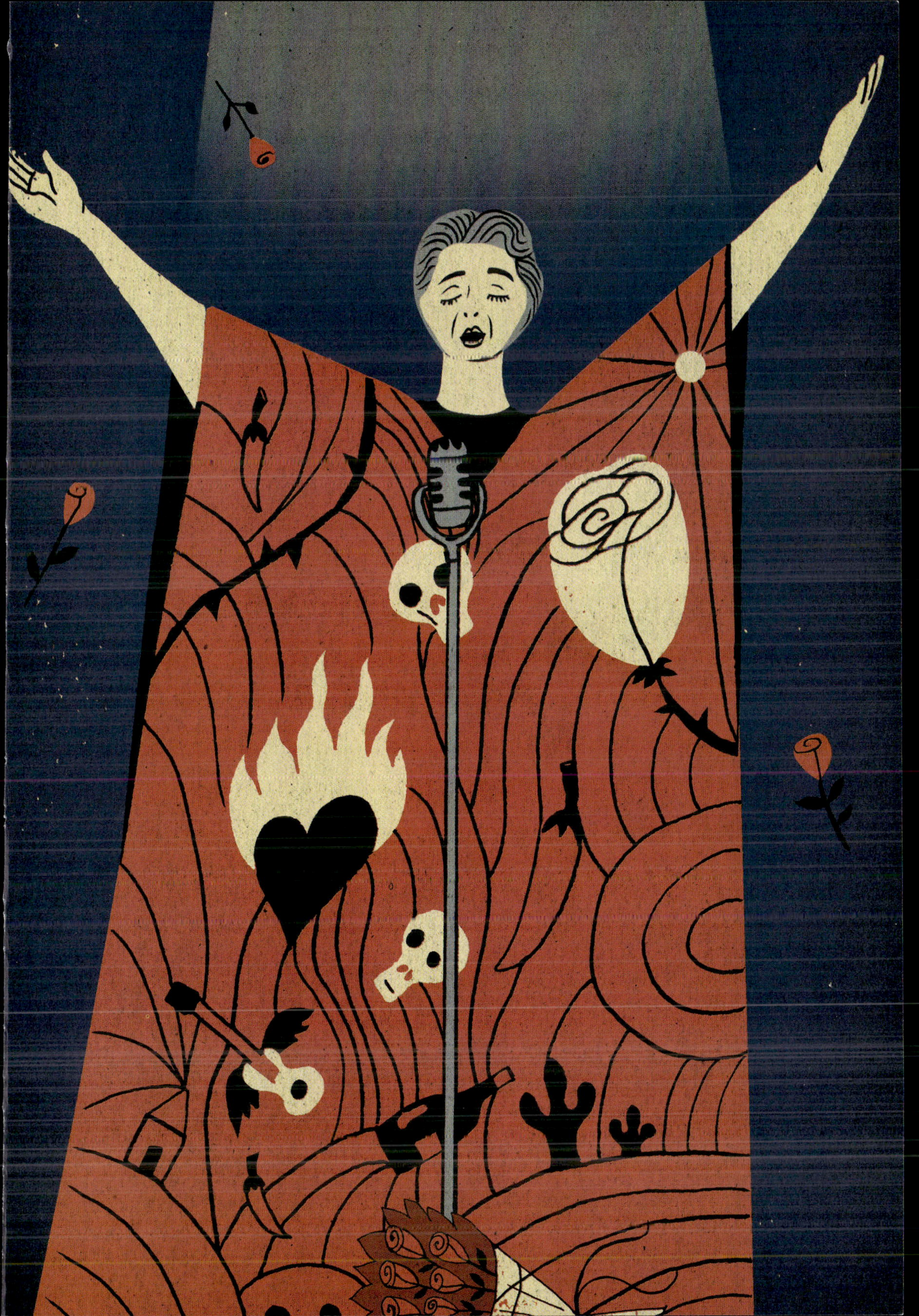

GABRIELA MISTRAL

(1889–1945)

Gabriela Mistral nació en Vicuña, Chile. Sus padres eran maestros y Mistral tuvo que superar dificultades de aprendizaje cuando era niña para más tarde convertirse en maestra a los 15 años. Fue una escritora prolífica y diplomática. En 1945 se convirtió en la primera latinoamericana en ganar el Premio Nobel de Literatura.

Gabriela Mistral was born in Vicuña, Chile. Raised by a family of teachers, Mistral overcame learning difficulties as a child to become a teacher herself at the age of 15. She became a prolific writer and diplomat. In 1945 she became the first Latin American woman to win a Nobel Prize in Literature.

Muchas de las cosas que hemos menester tienen espera, el Niño, no.... A él, no se le puede responder: "Mañana". Él se llama "Ahora".

Many things can wait....
But the child can't. You can't answer to him
"Tomorrow." His name is "Now."

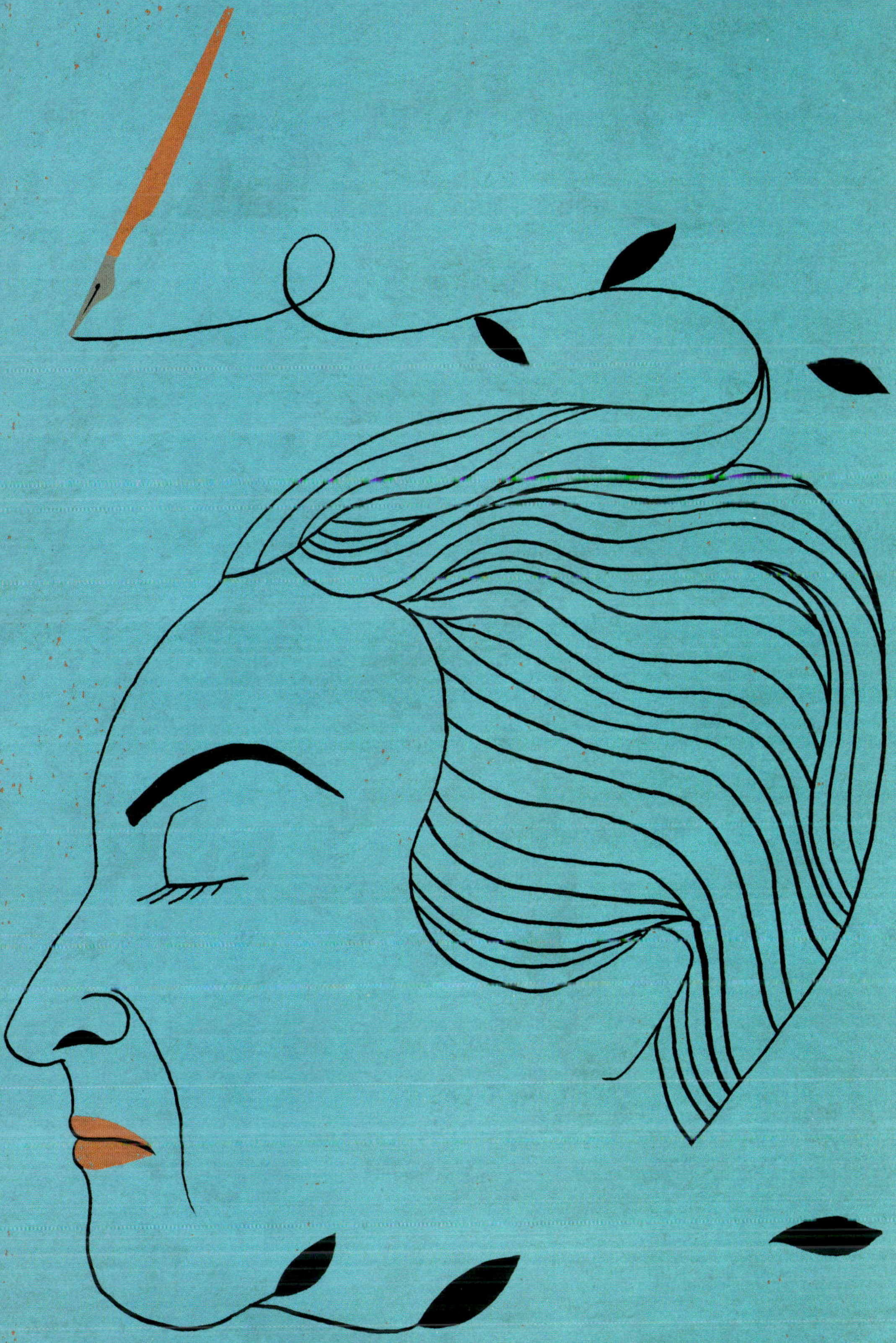

SOR JUANA INÉS DE LA CRUZ

(1651–1695)

Sor Juana nació en San Miguel Nepantla, un pequeño pueblo en México. Ella fue poeta, ensayista y monja. A lo largo de su vida defendió el derecho de las mujeres a la educación y es considerada un ícono feminista.

Born in San Miguel Nepantla, a small town in Mexico, Sor Juana was a poet, essayist, and nun. Throughout her life she defended women's access to education and is considered a feminist icon.

Yo no estudio para escribir … sino sólo por ver si con estudiar ignoro menos.

I do not study in order to write … but rather only to see if by studying I am ignorant of less.

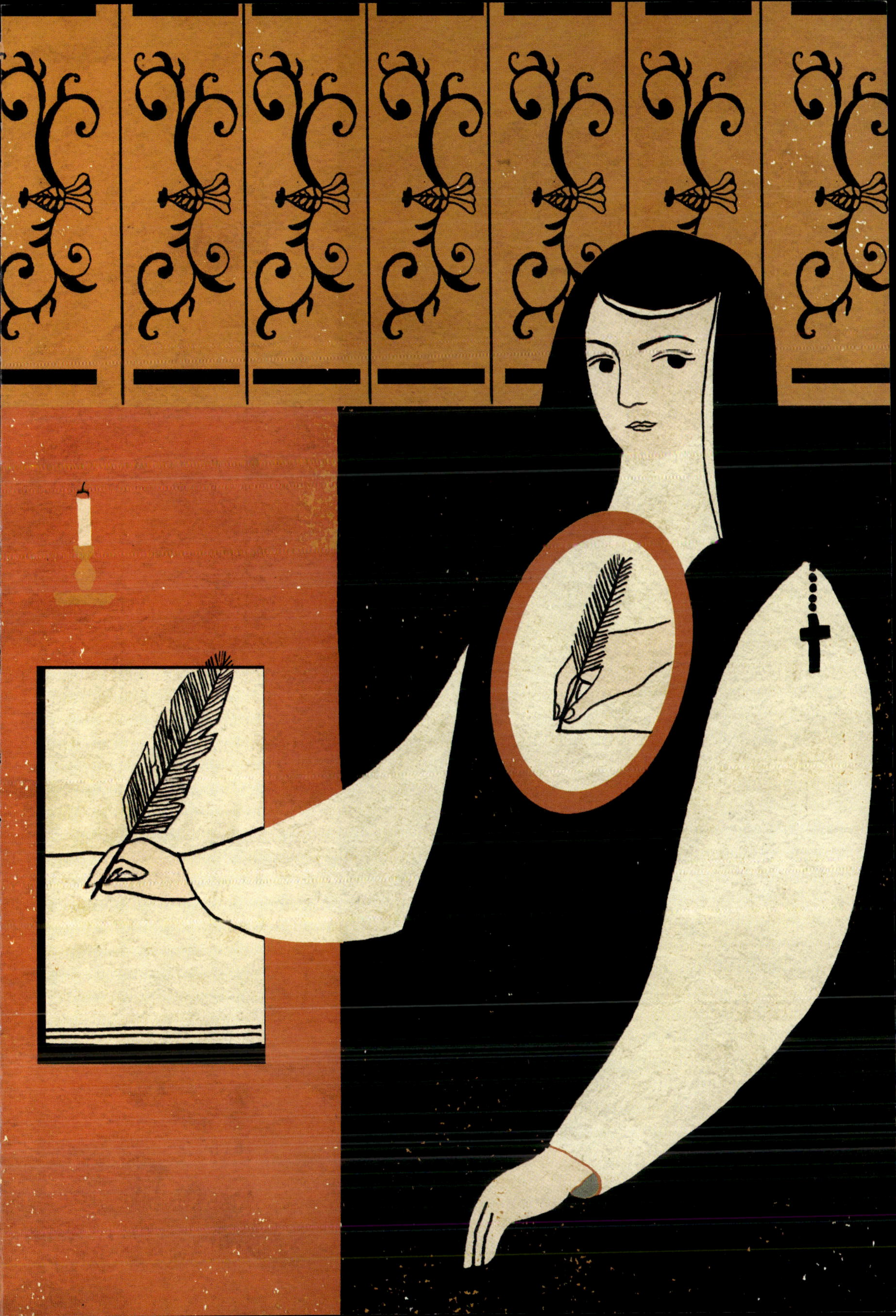

VIOLETA PARRA

(1917–1967)

Violeta Parra nació en San Carlos, Chile y mostró interés en escribir música y tocar la guitarra desde pequeña. Parra fundó el movimiento de la *Nueva Canción* que reflejaba su compromiso con la justicia social y la preservación de la cultura chilena.

Violeta Parra was born in San Carlos, Chile, and showed interest in writing music and playing guitar from a young age. Parra was a founder of the *Nueva Canción* (New Song) movement, which reflected her commitment to social justice and the preservation of Chilean culture.

Gracias a la vida que me ha dado tanto
Me ha dado la risa y me ha dado el llanto

Thank you to life, which has given me so much
It has given me laughter and it has given me tears

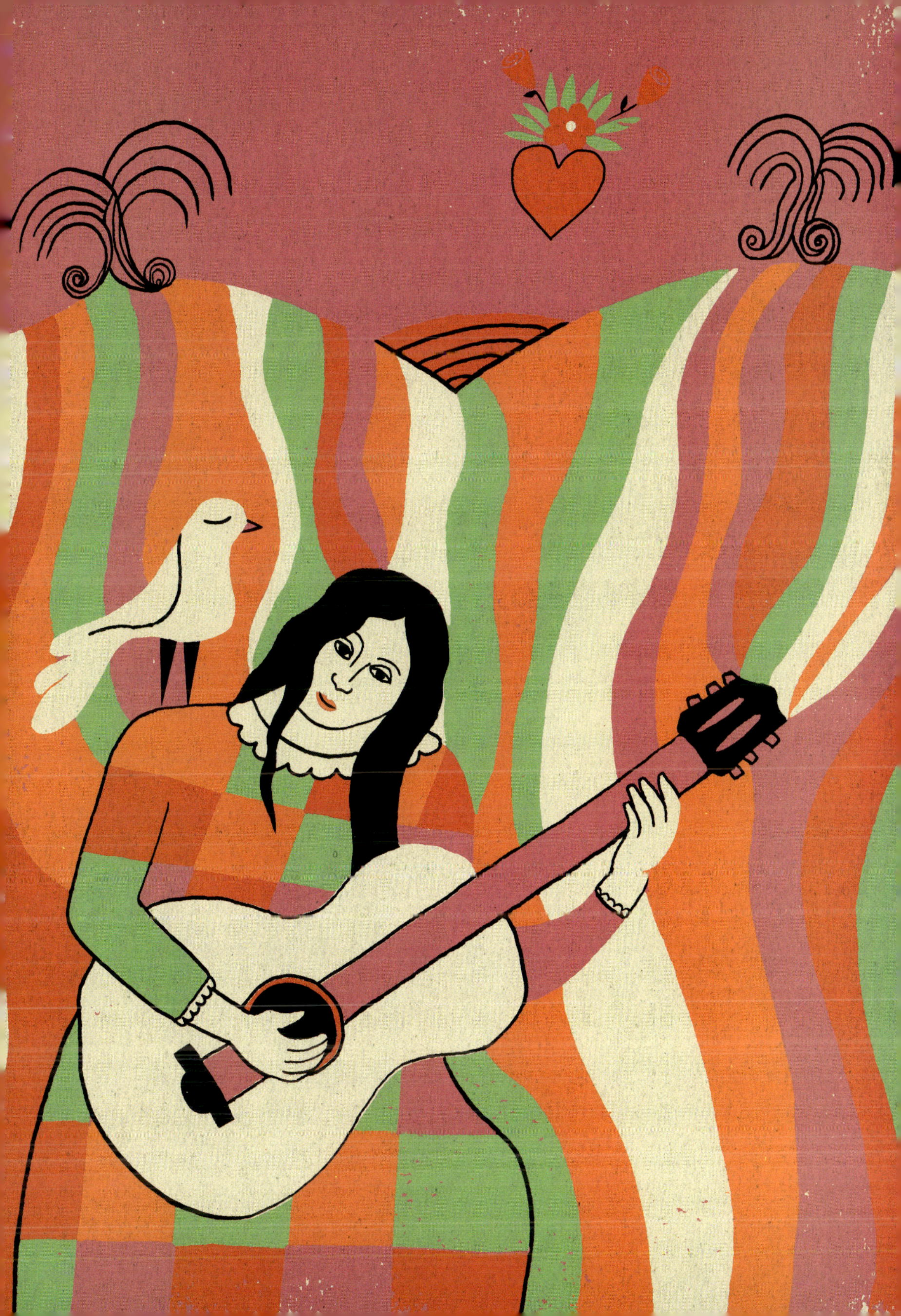

DOLORES HUERTA

(1930)

Dolores Huerta nació en Dawson, Nuevo México. Fue maestra y activista en defensa de los derechos de los trabajadores agrícolas. Huerta fundó el *United Farm Workers* con César Chávez para mejorar las condiciones de los trabajadores agrícolas.

Dolores Huerta was born in Dawson, New Mexico. She was a teacher and an activist for agricultural workers' rights. Huerta founded the United Farm Workers with César Chávez to improve the conditions of agricultural workers.

Cada momento es una oportunidad para organizar, cada persona es un activista en potencia, cada minuto una oportunidad para cambiar el mundo.

Every moment is an organizing opportunity, every person a potential activist, every minute a chance to change the world.

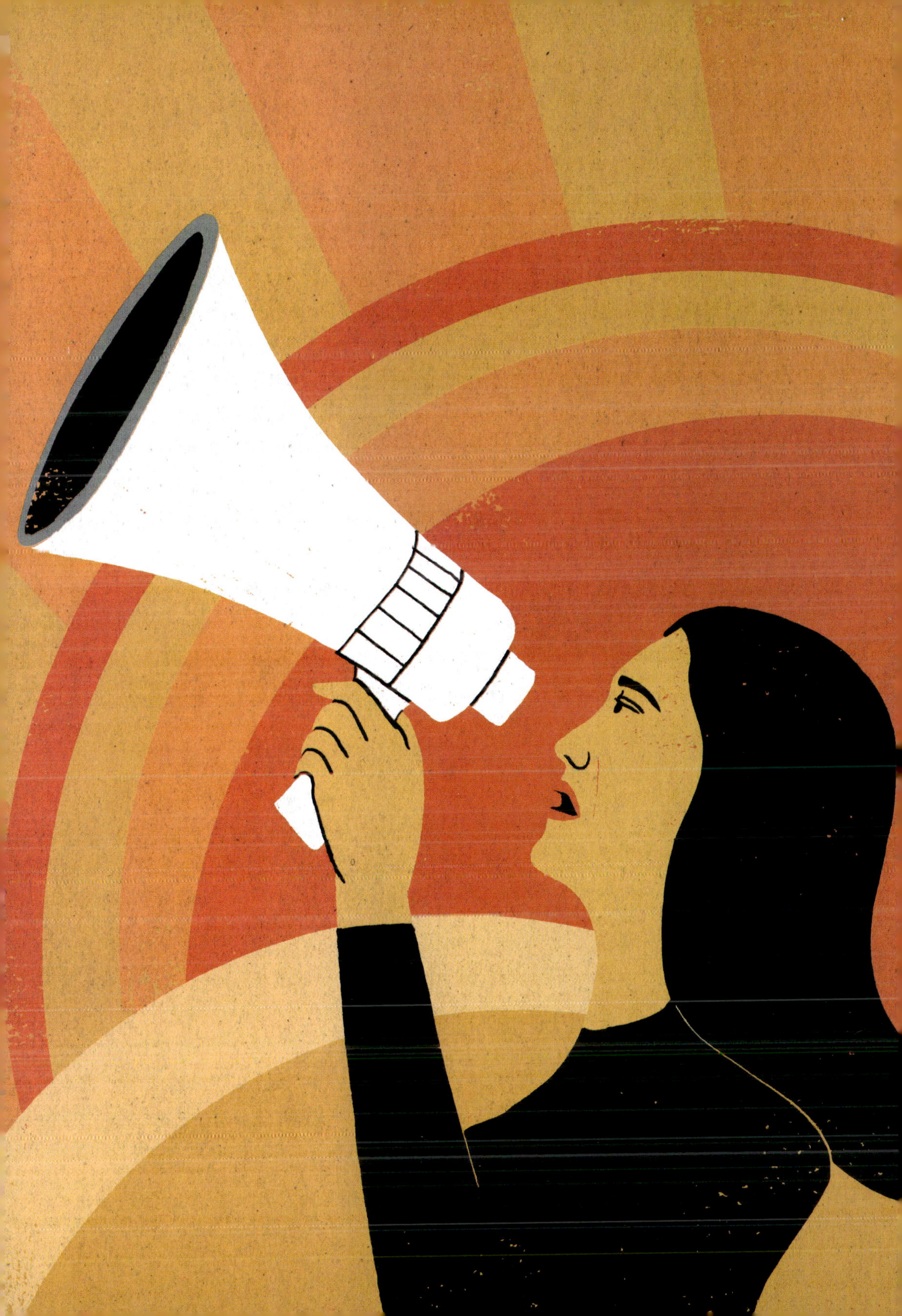

SARA GÓMEZ

(1942–1974)

Sara Gómez fue una cineasta nacida en La Habana, Cuba. Ella fue una de las pocas directoras de cine afro-cubanas que trabajó en un estilo documental que relataba narrativas que desafiaban los estereotipos de las mujeres y los afro-cubanos.

Sara Gómez was a filmmaker born in Havana, Cuba. She was one of the few Afro-Cuban female directors, working on documentary-style storytelling with fictional narratives that challenged stereotypical images of women and Afro-Cubans.

Me niego rotundamente
a quedarme callada.

I refuse to remain silent.

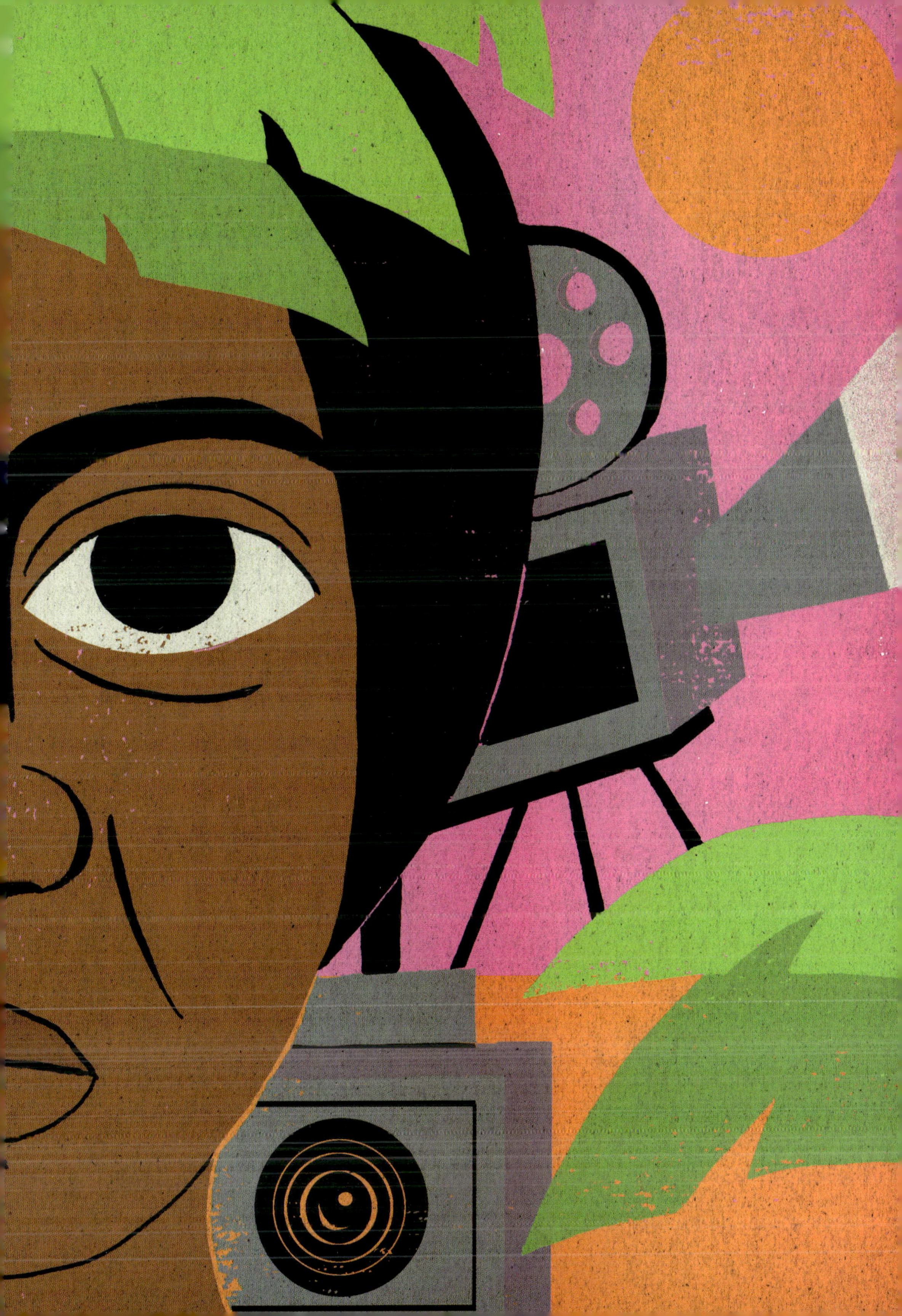

LOLA ÁLVAREZ BRAVO

(1907-1993)

Lola Álvarez Bravo nació en Lagos de Moreno, México. Se le considera una de las mejores fotógrafas de México y su trabajo ha dado la vuelta al mundo. Las imágenes de Bravo retratan la realidad de su país.

Lola Alvarez Bravo was born in Lagos de Moreno, Mexico. She is considered one of Mexico's best photographers and her work has traveled around the world. Bravo's images are a portrait of the reality of her country.

Si algo resulta útil de mi fotografía,
será en el sentido de ser una crónica
de mi país, de mi tiempo, de mi gente.

If my photographs serve any purpose,
they'll be a chronicle of my country,
my time, my people.

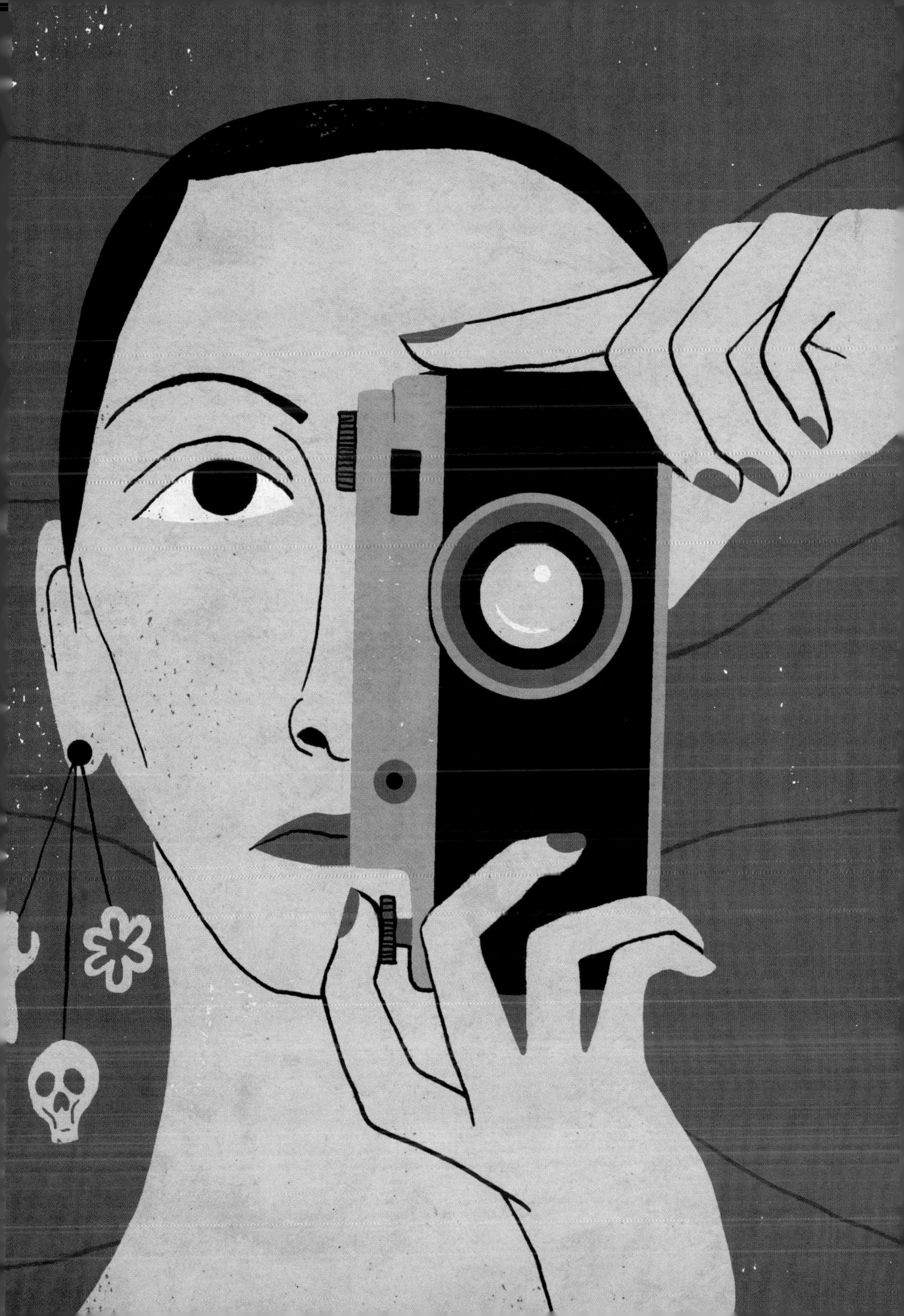

Illustrator
Hanna Barczyk is an award-winning illustrator who works with major publications and other institutional clients. Her work has been published in *The New Yorker*, *The New York Times*, Penguin/Random House books, and *The Economist* among others. In her artwork Hanna combines a variety of tools including pen and ink, acrylic paint, woodblock, and digital. When not illustrating she loves to dance salsa and tango, do yoga, read, and travel.

Writer
Tess Van Den Hurk-Moran is from Iowa, where she currently studies English and Spanish at the University of Iowa. She loves travel and learning about different cultures. All of the women in this book inspire her, and she is excited to share their stories.

Designer
Angie Vasquez is a graphic designer who loves color, travel, and food. She is from Colombia and lives in New York. She has two adorable pugs and when she's not designing she's usually cooking.

Illustration Copyright © 2019 by Hanna Barczyk

Nobel Lectures, Peace 1991-1995 © The Nobel Foundation 1992

A Julia de Burgos © 1938 by Julia de Burgos

The Stories I Read to the Children: The Life and Writing of Pura Belpré, the Legendary Storyteller, Children's Author, and New York Public Librarian © 2013 by Center for Puerto Rican Studies, Hunter College of the City University of New York

Las Cosas Simples © 1996 by Warner Music

Llamado por el Niño © 1948 by Gabriela Mistral Foundation, Inc.

Respuesta a Sor Filotea de la Cruz by Sor Juana Inés de la Cruz (1691)

Gracias a la Vida © 1966 by Violeta Parra

Election Day Is the Most Important Day of Your Life © 2016 by Huffington Post

Mi aporte © 1969 by Sara Gómez

Lola Alvarez Bravo: Recuento fotográfico © 1982 by Editorial Penélope

All rights reserved. Published by Scholastic Inc., *Publishers since 1920.* SCHOLASTIC and associated logos are trademarks and/or registered trademarks of Scholastic Inc.

The publisher does not have any control over and does not assume any responsibility for author or third-party websites or their content.

No part of this publication may be reproduced, stored in a retrieval system, or transmitted in any form or by any means, electronic, mechanical, photocopying, recording, or otherwise, without written permission of the publisher. For information regarding permission, write to Scholastic Inc., Attention: Permissions Department, 557 Broadway, New York, NY 10012.

ISBN 978-1-338-31661-2

10 9 8 7 6 5 4 3 2 1   19 20 21 22 23

Printed in the U.S.A.   40
First printing 2019

Cover and book design by Angie Vasquez

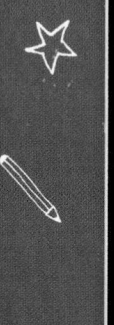

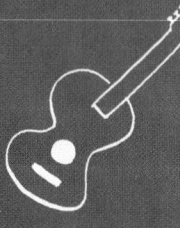

Illustration Copyright © 2019 by Hanna Barczyk

Nobel Lectures, Peace 1991-1995 © The Nobel Foundation 1992

A Julia de Burgos © 1938 by Julia de Burgos

The Stories I Read to the Children: The Life and Writing of Pura Belpré, the Legendary Storyteller, Children's Author, and New York Public Librarian © 2013 by Center for Puerto Rican Studies, Hunter College of the City University of New York

Las Cosas Simples © 1996 by Warner Music

Llamado por el Niño © 1948 by Gabriela Mistral Foundation, Inc.

Respuesta a Sor Filotea de la Cruz by Sor Juana Inés de la Cruz (1691)

Gracias a la Vida © 1966 by Violeta Parra

Election Day Is the Most Important Day of Your Life © 2016 by Huffington Post

Mi aporte © 1969 by Sara Gómez

Lola Alvarez Bravo: Recuento fotográfico © 1982 by Editorial Penélope

All rights reserved. Published by Scholastic Inc., *Publishers since 1920*. SCHOLASTIC and associated logos are trademarks and/or registered trademarks of Scholastic Inc.

The publisher does not have any control over and does not assume any responsibility for author or third-party websites or their content.

No part of this publication may be reproduced, stored in a retrieval system, or transmitted in any form or by any means, electronic, mechanical, photocopying, recording, or otherwise, without written permission of the publisher. For information regarding permission, write to Scholastic Inc., Attention: Permissions Department, 557 Broadway, New York, NY 10012.

ISBN 978-1-338-31661-2

10 9 8 7 6 5 4 3 2 1   19 20 21 22 23

Printed in the U.S.A.   40
First printing 2019

Cover and book design by Angie Vasquez